T0193615

A-Z SPIRITUALITY

Written by
JESSi PHAM

Illustrated by
DONiTA WHEELER

Balboa Press books may be ordered through booksellers or by contacting:

Balboa Press
A Division of Hay House
1663 Liberty Drive
Bloomington, IN 47403
www.balboapress.com
844-682-1282

Because of the dynamic nature of the Internet, any web addresses or links contained in this book may have changed since publication and may no longer be valid. The views expressed in this work are solely those of the author and do not necessarily reflect the views of the publisher, and the publisher hereby disclaims any responsibility for them.

Interior Image Credit: Donita Wheeler

ISBN: 979-8-7652-2514-1 (sc)
ISBN: 979-8-7652-2515-8 (e)

Library of Congress Control Number: 2022903211

Print information available on the last page.

Balboa Press rev. date: 03/25/2022

BALBOA.PRESS
A DIVISION OF HAY HOUSE

To My Daughter Aspen,

Always believe in
yourself and know
that you are Loved.

Mom

Angel

B
Blessing

Courage

D

Dreams

Emotions

Faith

G

Grateful

Hope

Imagination

J

Joy

Kindness

Love

M
Meditation

Nature

O

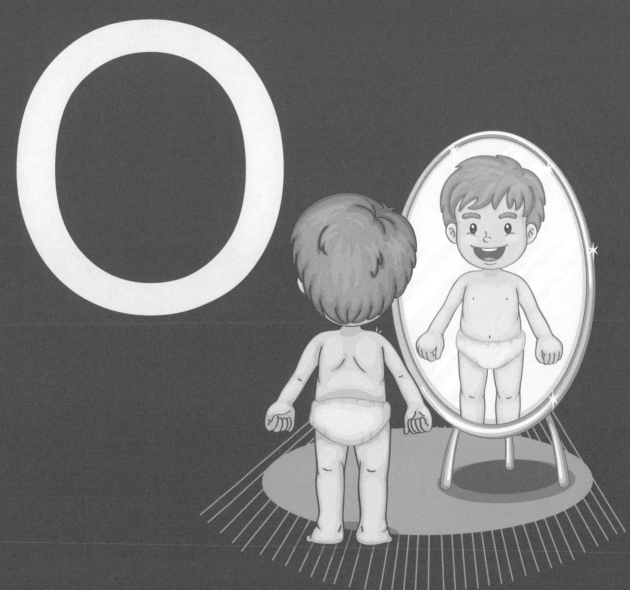

Ourselves

P

Peace

Quiet time

Rainbow

Spirit

Time

Universe

Voice

Wonder

23

Xx - Kisses

Yoga

Z

Zodiac

Printed in the United States
by Baker & Taylor Publisher Services